Start where you are.
Use what you have.
Do what you can.

—Arthur Ashe

zendoodle coloring

Uplifting Inspirations

Other great books in the series

zen**doodle** coloring

Calming Swirls

Cozy Cats

Creative Sensations

Enchanting Gardens

Inspiring Zendalas

Into the Forest

Tranquil Gardens

zendoodle coloring

Uplifting Inspirations

Quotable Sayings to Color and Display

illustrations by
Justine Lustig

ST. MARTIN'S GRIFFIN

NEW YORK

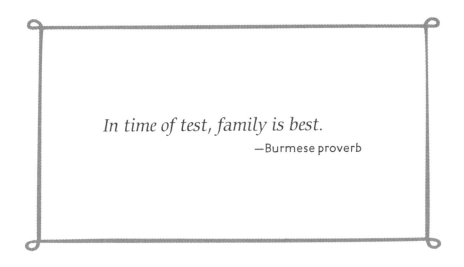

In time of test, family is best.

—Burmese proverb

ZENDOODLE COLORING: UPLIFTING INSPIRATIONS.
Copyright © 2016 by St. Martin's Press. All rights reserved.
Printed in the United States of America. For information, address
St. Martin's Press, 175 Fifth Avenue, New York, N.Y. 10010.

www.stmartins.com

ISBN 978-1-250-10901-9 (trade paperback)

Our books may be purchased in bulk for promotional, educational, or business use.
Please contact your local bookseller or the Macmillan Corporate and Premium
Sales Department at 1-800-221-7945, extension 5442, or by e-mail
at MacmillanSpecialMarkets@macmillan.com.

First Edition: May 2016

10 9 8 7 6 5 4

A heart that loves is always young.

—Greek proverb

Young
-AT-
heart

*We can complain because rose bushes
have thorns, or rejoice because
thorn bushes have roses.*

—Abraham Lincoln

Do one thing every day that scares you.

—Eleanor Roosevelt

I am bigger than the box I'm in.

—Rachel Cohn

The question isn't who is going to let me; it's who is going to stop me.

—Ayn Rand

In life, as in art, the beautiful
moves in curves.

—Edward G. Bulwer-Lytton

*To love and be loved is to feel
the sun from both sides.*

—David Viscott

To get the full value of joy you must have someone to divide it with.

—Mark Twain

Life isn't about finding yourself. Life is about creating yourself.

—George Bernard Shaw

Each morning we are born again. What we do today is what matters most.

—Buddha

Life without love is like a tree
without blossoms or fruit.

—Khalil Gibran

The purest and most thoughtful minds
are those which love color the most.

—John Ruskin

It ain't what they call you,
it's what you answer to.

—W. C. Fields

Accept that some days you are the pigeon,
and some days you are the statue.

—Scott Adams

Never love anyone who treats you like you're ordinary.

—Oscar Wilde

Love has no age, no limit;
and no death.

—John Galsworthy

Rebellion is the only thing that keeps you alive!

—Marianne Faithfull

Don't you dare underestimate the power of your own instinct.

—Barbara Corcoran

*In dreams and in love there
are no impossibilities.*

—Janos Arnay

Dwell on the beauty of life. Watch the stars,
and see yourself running with them.

—Marcus Aurelius

If your ship doesn't come in, swim out to it.

—Jonathan Winters

*Anyone who keeps the ability to
see beauty never grows old.*

—Franz Kafka

Life is too short for fake butter, cheese or people.

—unknown

The human race has only one really effective weapon and that is laughter.

—Mark Twain

Respect yourself and others will respect you.

—Confucius

Although the world is full of suffering, it is also full of the overcoming of it.

—Helen Keller

Being deeply loved by someone gives you strength, while loving someone deeply gives you courage.

—Lao Tzu

Keep your flame lit, and you will never feel darkness.

—J. Parker

For fast-acting relief, try slowing down.

—Lily Tomlin

The world is a book and those who do not travel read only one page.

—Saint Augustine of Hippo

*The friend who holds your hand and says
the wrong thing is made of dearer stuff
than the one who stays away.*

—Barbara Kingsolver

When you reach the end of your rope,
tie a knot in it and hang on.

—Franklin D. Roosevelt

A good laugh and a long sleep are the two best cures for anything.

—Irish proverb

Whoever is happy will make others happy too.

—Anne Frank

*Find something you're passionate about
and keep tremendously interested in it.*

—Julia Child

find **Joy** in all you do

How far that little candle throws his beams!
So shines a good deed in a weary world.

—William Shakespeare

Begin, be bold, and venture to be wise.

—Horace

Find ecstasy in life; the mere sense of living is joy enough.

—Emily Dickinson

Always be a first-rate version of yourself, instead of a second-rate version of somebody else.

—Judy Garland

We are all born for love.
It is the principle of existence
and its only end.

—Benjamin Disraeli

Ambition is a dream with a V8 engine.

—Elvis Presley

Time is a game played beautifully by children.

—Heraclitus

When your heart speaks, take good notes.

—Judith Campbell Exner

Be a rainbow in someone else's cloud.

—Maya Angelou

The best and most beautiful things in this world . . . must be felt with the heart.

—Helen Keller

Love is the greatest refreshment in life.

—Pablo Picasso

Yesterday is not ours to recover, but tomorrow is ours to win or lose.

—Lyndon B. Johnson

*When you arise in the morning think of
what a precious privilege it is to be alive—
to breathe, to think, to enjoy, to love . . .*

—Marcus Aurelius

*Love is a game that two
can play and both win.*

—Eva Gabor

For myself I am an optimist—it does not seem to be much use being anything else.

—Winston Churchill

Forever is composed of nows.

—Emily Dickinson

*One does not discover new lands
without consenting to lose sight of
the shore for a very long time.*
—André Gide

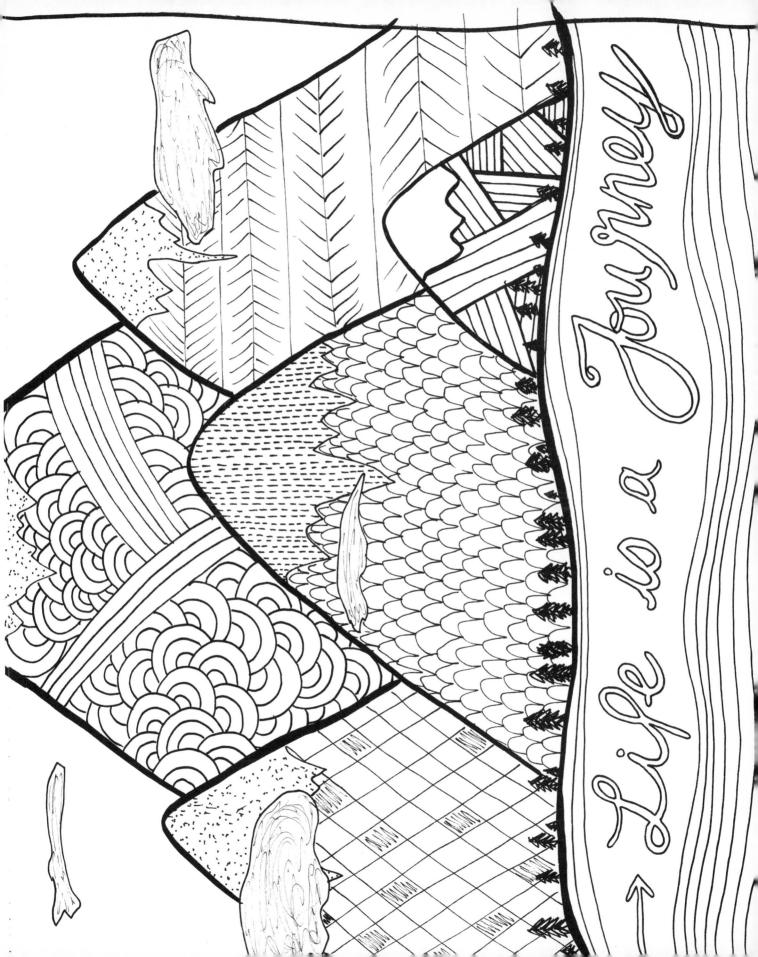

*We are all of us stars, and we
deserve to twinkle.*

—Marilyn Monroe

Courage is being scared to death but saddling up anyway.

—John Wayne

Hold fast to dreams,
For if dreams die
Life is a broken-winged bird,
That cannot fly.

—Langston Hughes

The two most important days in your life are the day you are born and the day you find out why.

—Mark Twain

It doesn't hurt to be optimistic.
You can always cry later.

—Lucimar Santos de Lima

Never do things others can do and will do, if there are things others cannot do or will not do.

—Amelia Earhart

Folks are usually about as happy as they make their minds up to be.

—Abraham Lincoln

It is what it is.

In the depth of winter, I finally learned that within me there lay an invincible summer.

—Albert Camus

Do anything, but let it produce joy.

—Walt Whitman